DISCOURSE THREE:

Organizational Leadership – An Essay On The Key Components For The Integration Of Technology While Leading In Increasingly Technologically Based Organizations

By

Yannique Thomas

Printed in the United States of America

Discourse Three: Organizational Leadership – An Essay On The Key Components For The Integration of Technology While Leading In Increasingly Technologically Based Organizations.

ISBN-13: 978-1-257-10733-9
ISBN-10: 1-257-10733-9

Lulu Enterprises, Inc.
3101 Hillsborough Street
Raleigh, NC 27607

Author

Yannique Angelique Helena (Whylly) Thomas is the youngest of six siblings from Adrianna Whylly and Vivian Whylly Sr. She holds a Bachelor of Arts degree in International Studies from Barry University, a Master of Arts degree in International Relations from University of Oklahoma, and an Advanced Post-Graduate Certificate in Organization and Management, Leadership specialization from Capella University. Currently she is working on completing her PHD in Organization and Management, specialization Leadership from Capella University.

Dedication

To my extraordinary mother, Adrianna (McKinney) Whylly. I could never have become anything without your example. You are my hero and everything that I could ever hope to become. It would not be possible for me to be who I am today with out your love, support, urging me to embrace my uniqueness and to keep moving forward. Thank you for always reminding me that the sky is the limit; that I could become anything that I set my mind to become; that I could accomplish anything that I wanted to accomplish as long as I am willing to work hard for it.

To my siblings…Denise (deceased), Michaela, Linda, Vivian, Jr., and Paul (deceased), thank you for leading the way for me and all your encouraging words.

To the rest of my family and friends, thank you for your love and support.

Contents

Author

Dedication

Chapter One

Introduction

Chapter Two

Chapter Three

Chapter One

Components of Leadership

Introduction

Researching findings suggest that the issue of leadership has been an ongoing discussion for decades (Bennis & Nanus, 1997). Researching data conclude that leadership development is a big trend and an investment worth taking (Bohn & Grofton, 2002). For scholars the standards of leadership that are definitive presently may not be so over time (Bennis & Nanus, 1997). Research findings suggest that it is necessary to review key components in order to keep pace with integrating immerging technology (Bohn & Grofton, 2002).

This essay will attempt to investigate and analyze existing literature on integration of technology as it applies to organizational leadership and present key components that leaders will need to understand and embrace in order to "lead" in increasingly technologically based organization.

Leading In Increasingly Technologically Based Organization

Leading In Increasingly Technologically Based Organization

The key elements that are necessary for leaders to understand and embrace in order to lead in an increasingly technologically based organization are boundless. Research data imply that leaders face many challenges when integrating technology. As a result there can no longer be the expectation of living in a society where the leader alone is expected to know the answers to every problem (Heiftz & Laurie, 2003).

For scholars a crucible principal for leaders to embrace in an increasingly technologically based organizations is that leadership and leading is emergent. Research data reflect that it is imperative for organizational leaders to stay relevant with the technology of time, era and environment that they are apart of (Scott, 2009).

Leadership Defined

Leadership Defined

For scholars every organization consists of players, goals and results. Research data suggest that leadership is an effective means to achieving those desired end results. Leadership is defined as the method by which a person motivates a group or an individual to realize an objective (Northouse, 2007).

For other scholars leadership is stimulating those that are following to achieve a specific intent (Phillips, 1992). Research data imply that the target symbolizes the ideals and inspiration of the leader. For other scholars the sheer brilliance is in how the leader interprets the followers' behavior response and how that affects the leaders' response (Burns, 1978).

Situational Leadership

Situational Leadership

For some scholars what determines the appropriateness of one approach from another approach is given the situation and the maturity level of the followers in relation to the specific task that the leader is attempting to accomplish through those following (Bolden et al., 2003; Hershey and Blanchard, 1977). Research findings suggest that leaders in increasingly technologically based organizations may have to ascertain the appropriate leadership approach when integrating technology (Hershey, Blanchard & Johnson, 2001).

Authentic Leadership

Authentic Leadership

The next key component for leading in an increasingly technological age is for leaders to lead authentically. Research has shown that it is critical for leadership success for leaders to be self-designers. When the leader follows his internal compass he is said to be leading authentically (George & Sims, 2007). Organizational leaders when integrating technology must become self-inventive (Kouzes & Posner, 2002). Research data suggest that leadership education may assist in developing skills (Bennis, 2003); but in order to be taken seriously, the organizational leader has to find out how to convey that genuine leadership talent that is distinctive to them (Kouzes & Posner, 2002).

Transformational Leadership

Transformational Leadership

In order to meet the challenges of organizational leadership in our changing times, transformational leadership is essential for the integration of technology (Bass, 1985). Transformational leadership is defined as:

> a process when one or more persons engage with others in such a way that leaders and followers raise one another to higher levels of motivation and morality…Though their purposes, which might have started out as separate but related, become fused (Burns, 1978, p.20).

Research data suggest that transformational leadership is materialized from the human condition for significance. It is engrossed in the human elements of reason ethics, principles and moral code. It surpasses routine connection with its focus transfixed on long term strategies. It liberates individual possibilities that modernize task and goals that ally with central components that emphasize the ideals and objectives overall (Covey, 1999).

For other scholars transformational leadership occurs when the leader formulates a system that persuades the follower to aspire to a higher level of moral consciousness that results in denial of self-interest to achieve the greater good (Bolden, Gosling, Maturano, & Dennison, 2003).

Research data indicates that transactional leadership continues to be the representation of those organizations that have chosen not to embrace the transformational role required to lead in an increasingly technologically based organization (Bolden et al., 2003; Northouse, 2007).

For some scholars the goal of transformational leadership is to effect long-term changes while genuinely changing people and organizations values, belief systems and behavior (Bolden et al, 2003). For other scholars transformational leadership is the capacity to produce the desire in others to be led, challenged and change (Hall, Johnson, Wysocki & Kepner, 2002).

Leadership Vision

Leadership Vision

Another key component for leading in an increasingly technologically based organization is for organizational leadership to have a leadership vision. In others words, organizational leadership must know where they are going (Bennis, 2003; Kotter, 2008). Research findings suggest that leadership vision can invent and create an environment that can empower employees to satisfy organizational needs (Bennis & Nanus, 1997). Research data suggest that it is the leaders' role to lift followers out of their everyday selves up to a higher level of awareness, motivation and commitment (Phillip, 1992).

Leadership Style

Leadership Style

For other scholars another key component for organizational leadership to embrace in integrating technology is that leaders must be required to possess the sophistication to understand which transformational leadership style is most appropriate given the situation (Bass & Avolio, 1994; Conger, 2004).

Bass and Avolio (1994) suggest five transformational styles. The first transformative approach is that the leader's behavior is idealized. In other words the leader's behavior is put on a pedestal and even romanticized as he discusses their salient ideals and principles. The second transformative approach is that the leader's behavior is inspirational motivation. The leader's behavior is very encouraging as the leader emphasis the positive potential of the future. The third transformative approach is that the leader's behavior demonstrates intellectual stimulation. The leader continuously reassesses fundamental perspectives to ensure that there are applicable and relevant. The fourth transformative approach is that the leader's behavior demonstrates individualized consideration. The leader is determined to provide exclusive feedback through ongoing education and training. The fifth transformative style is idealized attributes. The leader ascribes allegiance to those followers that identify with them (Bass & Avolio, 1994).

Chapter Two

Integration of Technology

Integration of Technology

Integration of technology from an organizational leadership perspective exceeds the conventional concern of solely computers and telecommunications. Research data suggest that the integration of technology encompasses the course of actions, resources, and factors that have an effect on the organization success and the construction of its products and services to achieve it (Thompson, Strickland, & Gamblel, 2005).

Research findings suggest that a fundamental intent of organizational leadership is to create competitive advantage. It is the ultimate responsibility of organizational leadership to effectively integrate all aspects of technology to position the organization of which it leads to cultivate and sustain a competitive posture within the market place (Thompson et. al, 2005).

For some scholars the way that organizations attempt to achieve competitive advantage is through integration of technology and by leading organization change (Kotter, 1995; Porter, 1990). Research results indicate that some techniques to consider are incorporating strategy, leadership and developing learning organizations. Research data suggest that creating and encouraging learning organizations fosters the commitment necessary for success verses opposition. Research also suggests that leading change requires commitment rather than consensus from others (Kotter, 1995).

Strategy And The Integration of Technology

Strategy And The Integration of Technology

The concept of strategy is said to have first appeared in organization theory in the late 1950's as a military metaphor (Hatch & Cunliffe, 2007). Strategy defined is described as choosing what not to do and making trade-offs while competing (Porter, 1996). Strategy is both the initiation and execution of a plan for competitive advantage (Porter, 1990). Research findings suggest that strategy requires assertive and proactive leadership to discern appropriate market trends and act on them. When executed properly the return on investment for organizational stake holders are enormous even when considering the entire spectrum of requirements and reactions to organizational results (Thompson et al, 2005).

For other scholars strategy is concerned with the process that an organization employs to evaluate its connection to its environment while pursuing its objectives at the broadest level (Bourgeois III, 1980). Research data imply that a principal objective of strategy for integration of technology for organizational leadership is achieving operational effectiveness and competitive success (Porter, 1990). Research findings suggest that both operational effectiveness and competitive strategy are essential to organizational effectiveness but are very dissimilar. Operational effectiveness denotes executing comparable task above competitors, while competitive strategy is about being unique (Porter, 1990; Porter, 1996).

Research findings indicate that organizations face many challenges that can be solved through integration of technology. For some scholars applying technical expertise; retraining organizational members to learn new habits; change their attitudes; and adapt new organizational values are some of the strategies organizational leadership can exploit (Heiftz & Laurie, 2003; Kotter, 1995; Collins, 2009).

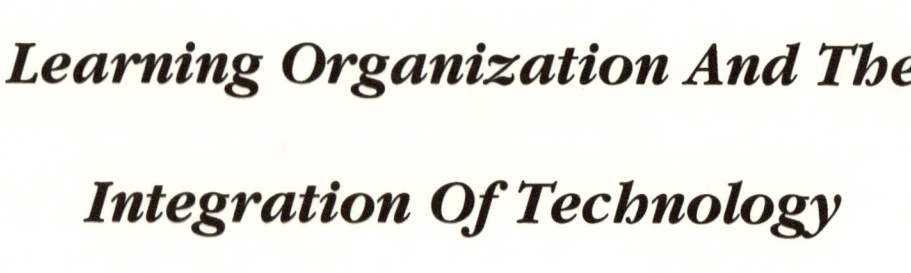

Learning Organization And The Integration Of Technology

Learning Organization And The Integration Of Technology

Research findings suggest that creating a learning organization is another strategy to integrate technology. The learning organization is defined as an environment where collective aspirations are free to explore until the desired result is achieved (Senge, 1990). Another definition proffered for the learning organization within an organization is to maintain or improve organization performance based on experience. The goal of the learning organization is to make changes to improve competitive advantage (Nevis, DiBella & Gould, 1995; Porter, 1990).

For other scholars researchers differ on the question of what is a learning organization. Advocates argue that there is no such thing as an authentic learning organization. It is only an ideal (Redding, 1997). Garvin (1993) view the learning organization as "an organization skilled at creating, acquiring and transferring knowledge, and at modifying its behavior to reflect new knowledge and insights" (p. 80).

Research data imply that it is the task of organizational leadership to examine the organization and determine what specific characteristics and technology are to be integrated for the organization to have competitive advantage. This is essential because there is no common design outlining the features of a learning organization (Redding, 1997).

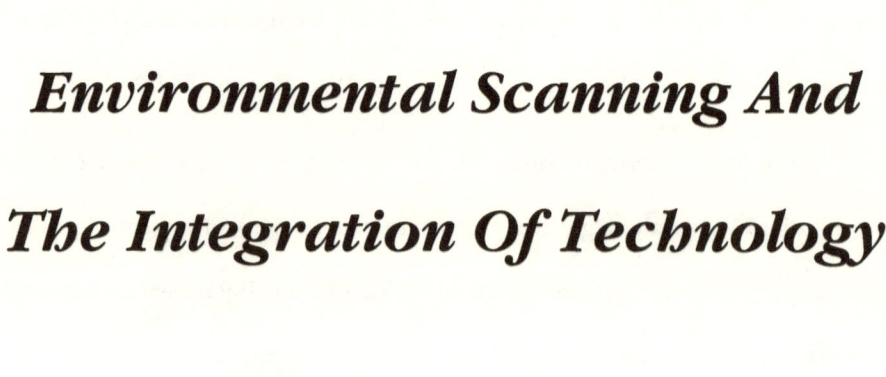

Environmental Scanning And

The Integration Of Technology

Environment Scanning And The Integration Of Technology

Environmental scanning is another strategy that organizational leadership may exploit to integrate technology. Research data indicates that environmental scanning is considered the fundamental method that establishes the organizational adaptation process (Sawyerr, Ebrahimi & Thibodeaux, 2000). It is commonly known as the first step in the process of linking the appropriate strategy and environment (Beal, 2000).

Research findings suggests that environmental scanning is explicitly recognized as a starting point of monitoring the external environment and collecting information of strategic importance for use in making organizational decision (Sawyerr, Ebrahimi & Thibodeaux, 2000). For other scholars research has found that despite the fact that an environment may favor a particular strategy other strategies can succeed (Hambrick, 1981).

Research findings suggest that by integrating technology through the manufacturing of techniques and approaches in to the framework of the organizations day to day operations, businesses can organize their ingenuity and learning more effectively (Garvin, 1993).

Communication And The

Integration Of Technology

Communication And The Integration Of Technology

Another key component for success that organizational leadership must understand and embrace when integrating technology is effective communication. Research evidence indicates that effective leadership is said to have occurred when the communication of leaders and subordinates is illustrated by shared confidence, respect and loyalty (Northouse, 2007).

Effective communication is a prerequisite for achieving organizational success in integration of technology. It is a key component that organizational leadership will need to understand and embrace. Research findings suggest that effective communication in leadership does not happen automatically (Yukl & Tracey 1992).

For some scholars leaders must communicate within the organization through channels that flow up, down or across organizational levels as well as outside of the organization. Communication may be informal or formal within or outside of the organization. The key concept is the fact that integration of technology requires communication to take place between an organization and its environment and within the organization (Gardner & Winder, 1999).

Emotional Intelligence (EI/EQ)

And The Integration Of

Technology

Emotional Intelligence (EI/EQ) And The Integration of Technology

For other scholars Emotional Intelligence (EI/EQ) is a key component that organizational leadership must understand and embrace for success. EI/EQ is considered one of the most important capabilities for leaders to develop. Emotional Intelligence is defined as the ability to motivate oneself and persist in the face of frustration while emphasizing hope. Research implies that leading in an increasingly technologically based organization may require constant change and barricading apprehension from inundating the leader's ability to think which is essential for organizational success (Goleman, 1998).

Chapter Three

Conclusion and Discussion

Conclusion

In conclusion, research has shown that transformational leadership is essential for organizational leadership to lead in an increasingly technologically based organization (Bass, 1985). For scholars transformational leaders employ strategies to embrace the development of their associates and ultimately optimize the development of the organization (Bass & Avolio, 1994).

I concur with Bennis (2003) that inclusive of all the value points that have been identified, organizational leaders must embrace and understand that effective integration of technology does not entail forcing plans and strategies on others; but empowering and enlisting participants to follow (Bennis, 2003).

I concur with Kotter (1995) that the basic goal of integration of technology as it applies to organizational leadership is to make fundamental changes in how business is conducted in order to help the organizational players cope with the evolving market systems (Kotter, 1995).

I agree with the notion that the successful integration of technology for organizational leadership is predicated on the organizations continual ability to exploit emerging opportunities as well as how well the organization responds to those observations and interpretation of the dynamic world in which it operates (Gupta & Govindarajan, 2002).

Discussion

Research findings suggest that transformational leadership is not due to charisma. Instead, it is thought to be a behavioral process capable of being learned (Tichy & Devanna, 1986). For other scholars the goal of transformational leadership is to transform people and organizations in a literal sense (Bass, 1985; Bolden et al., 2003).

Research data suggest that leadership is an art that cannot be taught in a classroom (Bennis, 2003; Hill, 2004). For other scholars a person does not have to be born with great leadership characteristics (Bennis, 2003; George & Sims, 2007). Research data suggest that it may be acquired by actively engaging in it by observing and interacting with others (Hill, 2004).

Bibliography

Bibliography

Beal, R.M. (2000). Competing effectively: Environmental scanning, competitive strategy, and organization performance in small manufacturing firms. *Journal of Small Business Management, 38* (1), 27-46.

Bourgeois, L.J.M III. (1980). Strategy and environment: A conceptual integration. *Academy of Management Review, 5*(1), 25-39.

Conger, J. (2004). Developing leadership capability: what's inside the black box? *Academy of Management Executive, 18*(3), 136-140.

Gardner, D., & Winder, C. (1998). Using benchmarking to improve organizational communication. *Quality Assurance, 6*, 201-211.

Garvin, D.A. (1993). Building a learning organization. *Harvard Business Review, 71*(4), 78-91.

Goleman, D. (1998). *Working with emotional intelligence*. New York: Bantam Books.

Gupta, A.K., & Govindarajan, V. (2002). Cultivating a global mindset. *Academy of Management Executive, 16*(1), 116-126. Retrieved from Business Source Complete database.

Hall, J., Johnson, S., Wysocki, A., & Kepner, K. (2002). Transactional Leadership: The Transformation of Managers and Associates. Retrieved from Business Source Complete database.

Hambrick, D.C. (1981). Environment, strategy, and power within top management teams. *Administrative Science Quarterly, 26*, 253-276.

Hatch, M.J., & Cunliffe, A.L. (2006). *Organization theory: Modern, symbolic and postmodern perspectives*. Oxford, UK: Oxford University press.

Heiftz, R.A., & Laurie, D.L. (2003).The leader as teacher: creating the learning environment. Retrieved on 11 January 2010 from, http://www.iveybusinessjournal.com/view_article.asp?intArticle_ID=395

Hershey, P., & Blanchard, K.H. (1997). *Management of organizational behavior*. Englewood Cliffs, NJ: Prentice Hall.

Hershey, P., Blanchard, K.H., & Johnson, D.E. (2001). *Management of organization behavior: leading human resources*. (8th e.d.). Upper Saddle River: Prentice Hall.

Hill, L. (2004). New manager development for the 21st century. *Academy of Management Executive, 18* (3), 121-126.

Nevis, E.C., DiBella, A.J., & Gould, J.M. (1995). Beyond the charismatic leader: Leadership and organizational change. *California Management Review,* 73-97.

Porter, M.E. (1990). The competitive advantage of nations. (cover story). *Harvard Business Review, 68*(2), 73-93. Retrieved from Business Source Complete data.

Porter, M.E. (1996). What is Strategy? *Harvard Business Review, 74*(6), 61-78. Retrieved from Business Source Complete database.

Redding, J. (1997). Hardwiring the learning organization. Training and Development, 51(8), 61-67.

Sawyerr, O.O., Ebrahimi, B.P., & Thibodeaux, M.S. (2000). Executive environmental scanning, information source utilization and firm performance: The case of Nigeria. *Journal of Applied Management Studies, 9* (1), 95-115.

Scott, S. (2009). *Fierce leadership: A bold alternative to the worst "best" practices of business today.* New York: Broadway Books.

Thompson, A., Strickland, A., & Gamble, J. (2005). *Crafting and executing strategy: Text and readings* (15th ed.). New York: McGraw-Hill.

Tichy, N., & Devanna, M. (1986). *Transformational Leadership:* New York: Wiley.

Yukl, G., & Tracey, B. (1992). Consequences of influence tactics used with subordinates, peers and the boss. *Journal of Applied Psychology,* 77, 525-535.

Appendix

Forms

Survey

TEN ESSENTIAL COMPONENTS OF LEADERSHIP

HOW DO YOU RATE AGAINST THE TEN ESSENTIAL COMPONENTS OF LEADERSHIP ON A SCALE OF 1 TO 3?

(3 = STRONG, 2= AVERAGE, 1=WEAK)

1. TOLERANCE   _____

2. HONESTY   _____

3. DETERMINATION   _____

4. PERSUSASION   _____

5. PLAN   _____

6. FOCUS   _____

7. OBSERVATION   _____

8. HAPPINESS   _____

9. SELF-CONFIDENCE   _____

10. DESIRE   _____

ADDITIONAL INFORMAITON

AGE   _____

GENDER   _____

HIGHEST EDUCATION   _____

OF UNDERGRADUATE LEADERSHIP COURSES TAKEN_____

Feed Back/Testimonial

Order Form

Yes! Please send me a copy of _____

Quantity	Item	Cost
_____	Discourse One: Lessons From My Mother On Leadership	$19.95
_____	_____	$_____
_____	_____	$_____
	Florida Residents add 6% sales tax	$1.20
	Shipping and Handling	$5.99
	TOTAL COST	$_____

Email:

_____

Name:

_____

Address:

_____

City_____State____Zip_____

__Check   __Money Order   _ Cash

_____

Available to speak at seminars, conferences and workshops by contacting

leadershiplessons1@gmail.com or writing to P. O. Box 48372, Tampa, FL

33646. Place orders by filing out form send via mail or email.

Please allow 4-6 weeks for delivery.

Index

Left Blank Intentionally

www.ingramcontent.com/pod-product-compliance
Lightning Source LLC
Chambersburg PA
CBHW021933170526
45157CB00005B/2307